Iconic Dreams

COLLECTION OF POEMS BY

STEVEN YELLON

First published by Busybird Publishing 2020

Copyright © 2020 Steven Yellon

ISBN 978-1-922465-21-4

This book is copyright. Apart from any fair dealing for the purposes of study, research, criticism, review, or as otherwise permitted under the Copyright Act, no part may be reproduced by any process without written permission. Enquiries should be made through the publisher.

Any person depicted by the contents, is by their own interpretation. The contents are a product of Steven Yellon's imagination

Cover design: Busybird Publishing

Layout and typesetting: Busybird Publishing

Busybird Publishing
2/118 Para Road
Montmorency, Victoria
Australia 3094
www.busybird.com.au

I, a London born construction professional composed this collection, which is a new territory for me. It may not follow classical rules of poetry; however, it facilitates expression and provokes questions seeking thought – for that I thank my imagination.

I would also like to thank my wife Lubna, daughters Michaela and Emaan for just being them, who I love, enjoy and annoy.

I acknowledge all my friends and foes, past and present, who have impacted my mind.

Fiona McIlory, the published Canberra poet, encouraged me and her input is appreciated.

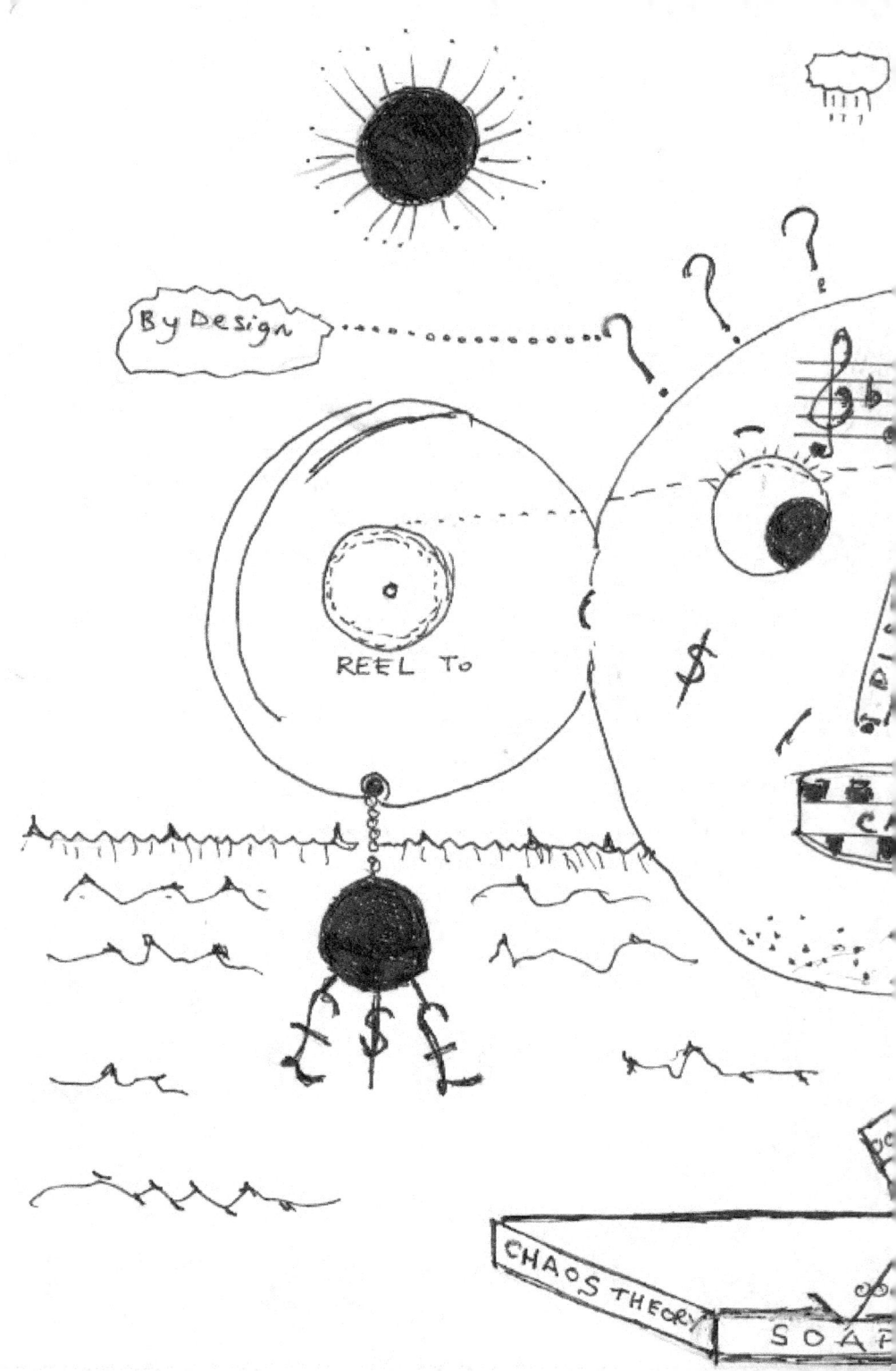

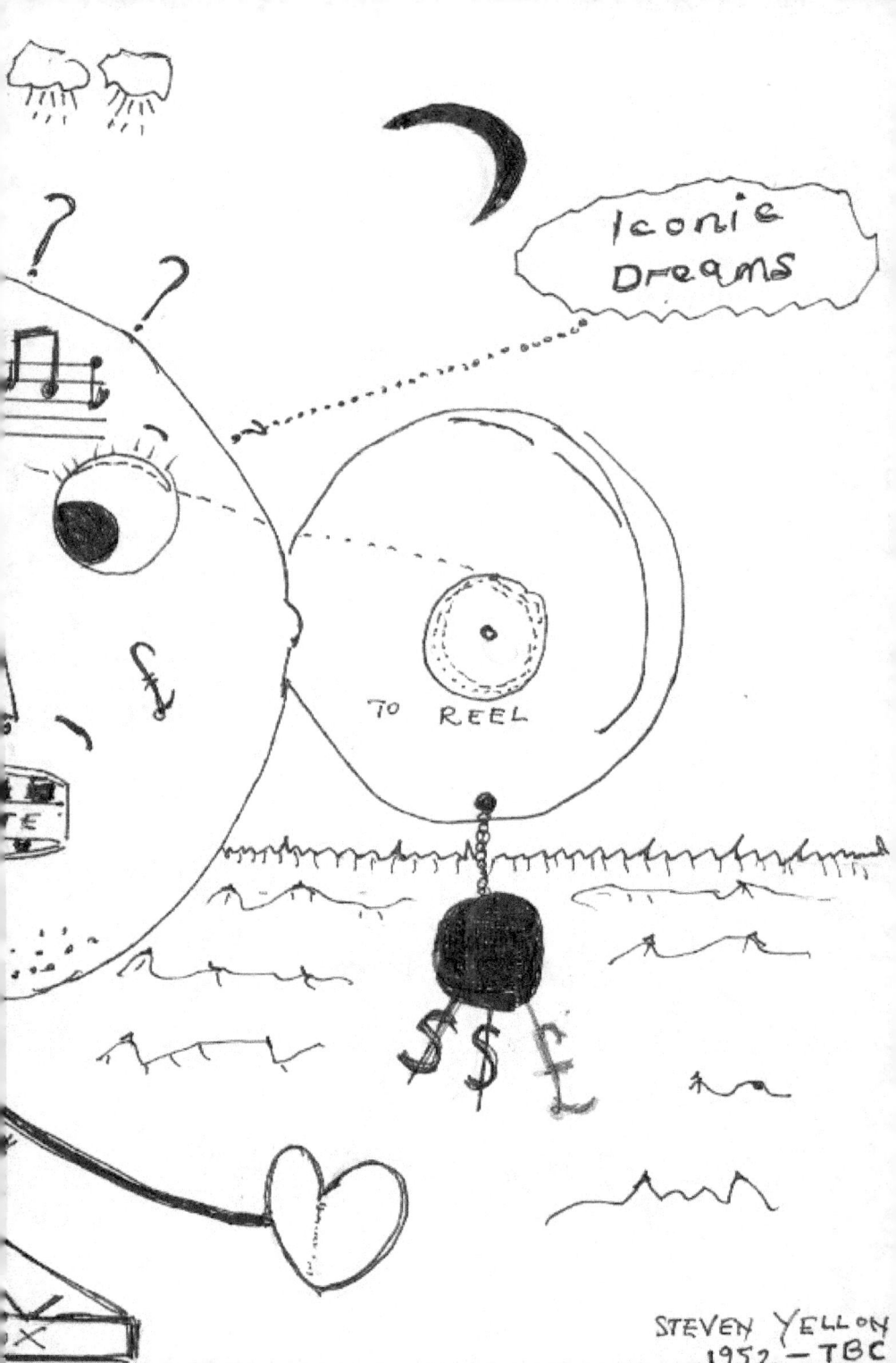

CONTENTS

INTRODUCTION	1
PART 1 - THOUGHTS	3
Catch a miracle	5
Deep blue	6
Magic mirror	7
Southern Cross	8
Dog walk	9
Out for the count	10
Grand fools	11
Avenue of dreams	12
Fight	13
The winds	14
Frontier	15
Anthem of hope	16
Greed and sin	18
The truth	19
PART 2 - SHADES OF LOVE	21
Sky and clouds	22
Regina	23
Hearts and spirits	24
By design	25
King and queen	26
While you were out	27
Joe her dream	28
Swing honey	29
Broken robot	30
Mother and child	31
Turn the key	32

PART 3 - REFLECTIONS OF THE MIND   33

Shut down our minds honey   34
You were a flower   35
Then and now   36
Betrayal and a thousand screams   37
Stupid man   38
Dreams come true   39
Peace   40
When truth was a gift   41
Evaporated love   42
Say goodbye   43

PART 4 - THE END AND BEYOND   45

Midnight blues   46
In life there is air   47
The world I saw   48
It's over my friend   49
The last soldier falls   50
True is not blue   51
Prelude of the end   52
Life   53
Beyond the stars   54
Seeing   55
Pagan   56

Introduction

Iarar – risk management

identify – the issue and I call my own SOS, with my tapping feet

acknowledgement – of my mistakes as I search my mind waiting for the jailer to greet

reflect – on the past and believe me in times like these requires no more lies

anticipate – the action of executioner's axe – my God I will soon meet

resulting – in certain death my head rolls giving the captive audience such a treat

PART 1

THOUGHTS

Catch a miracle

today, I tried to catch a rainbow and you tried to catch that cloud so white

yesterday, I tried to catch a single rain drop and you tried to capture the wind in sight

tomorrow, I try and catch the Sun, but that may be a task too much for me

you try and catch the Moon, it is there waiting, for you to see

if we are successful and catch these life symbols, it would be an achievement so great

when we succeed in this miracle – let us dwell where it will take us, to a higher state

we then can both catch our spirits, which would be an act so well done

followed by searching, for our souls, which would be extreme fun

dreaming is a day to day pastime for me and you to explore

fantasies are reality, I know, I hope, for more

it just needs commitment in adversity – believe me, I saw

Deep blue

in a world of horror I scream and dishonour I dream

in a war I run

with greed, I have no fun

in a surreal world, I look and stare, with fools, I despair

think of oxygen so light, pure

with the future, it may be bright

no harm can occur, be brave, life adds up to nought

have just desires and only transparent thought

Magic mirror

in the magic mirror house of fun
stand up in line, laughter until it is done
try and play the game we all know
kids, adults, the same every show

test your imagination – it is free
pretend I am you and you are me
jump in front of the mirror so cool
for a moment act like a strange fool

big belly now a head like a monster man
looking up to the roof, fat then thin
a game like an acid trip it takes no pills
bringing back memories, my photographic stills

people distorted rather strange to see
the bearded lady looks a real drag – let it be
hearing laughter, fun for me
the exit is now near – what a surprise
time for reality and open one's eyes

Southern Cross

the sun is so glaring, straight in my eyes
I am so happy I must say
I am overjoyed, life going my way

the sky is clear tonight
I am relaxed the stars are so bright
I am surprised life is going without a fight

I walk tall moonlight beam
the Southern Cross reflecting everywhere
I realise the sand dunes are very deep
but in my heart, I just do not care

Dog walk

I have been awake, but sleeping too
together is fine, the sky is a reddish blue
I went for a walk today, dog in tow, with my secret dreams
down by the still lake where the stream flows forth
the air is so very clean and there are not many flies
my mind so clear, devoid of the world's lies
I hear in the distance, back up the hill, the Buddhists chant
with their cries of despair, in a world full of want
now silent and so serene in their robes so plain
their God is my God, even if my mind seeks gain

Out for the count

I have been out for the count today
knocked from pillar to post
never seen such thuggery in this way
the winner was smirking and drinking his toast
battered black and blue, muscles so raw
gasping for air as the crowds cry for more
on the ropes, I hear them so clear
as I go down my head hits the canvas, I fear
blood dripping from my cut so deep
vibrations of clapping stop me getting to my feet
gumshield smashed crunched and flew a long way
oh my God it's over for me
there is nothing more to say

Grand fools

I am on stage looking down on all of you
famous, rich, and drugged – you are just the paying fools
let me hit my beat hard, the drumsticks are my tools
now, let your minds trip so far you can clap me too much –
you grand fools

I am on stage looking down on all of you
happy stoned on my white pills and the others that look bright and blue
let my synthesiser grasp your minds as you cheer – this song is so new
now let you imagination expand so wide – I can enter every thought –
you grand fools

I am on stage looking down on all of you
the light show is great too – every colour of a rainbow in the sky
red, white and blue – colours of my flag at home, the home I left, I shudder why
now let your thoughts, they are so elastic, stretch – you grand fools

Avenue of dreams

I travel so fast, down the avenue of dreams

a simple journey, where reality and imagination meet, it seems

as the Sun goes down, the heat retracts

all I see is the fools it appears

egos puffed up, intelligence devoid

but land as vast, as I race the gears

as the Moon rises and the winds commence, all I see is good people it appears

meek and mild, intelligence so humble, land so small, as I brake the gears

stop – breathe the air, flies too much to impede my rest, do I care

dreams are there for me, as I write myself in the rocks, for followers to stare

now, let's consider carefully, the future may be simple and hopefully fair

I trust the next generation to read the past life, improve their life, if they dare

Fight

I am not a fish as I just do not like water
never scared to show my face in any quarter
if there was a war today, I would run from the slaughter
killing the men, I just cannot, my gun will falter

I am not a coward, no, not a coward, never call me yellow belly

I am not slow to state the facts – don't confuse me with the others
dead fish do not suck for air anymore – despair for their mothers
never scared to compose my latent thoughts
in a battle of war, no guns, only words to fight invading thoughts

I am not a coward, no, not a coward, never call me yellow belly

tears run to create a stream, pure needing no clarity
inviting fish, tricking them into being caught – show no sanity
prepare the salt beds and smoke grills – images of such deceit
the wire, set the trap now, wound into the ultimate surrender
and retreat.

I am not a coward, no, not a coward, never call me yellow belly

The winds

the winds blow across the desert plains, bringing swarms of insects to our doors

where there is no water or food, the ravens fly high, silhouette under the Moon

friends here in this tent devoid of cheats, liars and whores

the boys will go to fight the war, let's pray for our return to this room

we fight the bombs, with just our sharp swords to win this war

leather bags, heavy of our gold is the only reward, and all is our doom

if our bodies return stiff, dead, stack them high to illustrate the politicians flaw

the winds take out the truth, echoing in my mind

the fight is all about our land barren, depleted and no value to the invading gang

the kingdom is there for the winners reward, I just hope they are kind

they may strut, brazen, but bloodied for the losers to hang

we will fight their propaganda, blasting out from the speakers, by closing our ears

their leader if he wins, has his mouth open, teeth like deadly snakes fangs

will they destroy all that remains?

will they listen to the mothers and children's pleading fears?

Frontier

I saw the frontier today in the distant haze

however, I was amazed by the clarity of view, across the barbed wire

stumbling with no coherent plan, in the heat and totally fazed

I approached the barbed wire, wall of hate, not knowing if the gate was locked

tip toeing impossible as my legs deprived of oxygen, had gone to sleep

I admit now the guard looked fierce, hand on trigger, I was so shocked

he pointed the barrel at the centre of my temple

pushing the hot steel on my frown as my children weep

yes, I admit the frontier was so near, but alas so far, as the gate was locked

Anthem of hope

someone wants a concession of my mind and soul so they can own me

in this closed ghetto of shame the cold winds blow off the Baltic Sea

the snow is so virginal it shows all the footsteps as the soldiers flee

snow melted not by the sun, but by the warm blood that flows from corpses I see

I refuse to give them what they want, that is my chant, my anthem of hope – love not blood

I will never let this corrupt state win this brutal war

I may be poor and with just this shelter as my refuge, not even with a door

it is my life, I stand proud and tall, I will never grovel on the floor

I refuse to give them what they want, that is my chant, my anthem of hope – love not blood

they want to change my religion too – I refuse to give them my birthright

my gold teeth, they would rip them out, I alive, would scream and shout their major, a disgusting human, he thinks he is so tall but in my eyes he is stout

he drinks much wine, I hope he gets infested by a whore and suffers painful gout

I refuse to give them what they want, that is my chant, my anthem of hope – love not blood

caress of warm Mediterranean winds never get up this far, it's a shame

the warmth was my family stolen, by design that was their game

I will die one day – an event witnessed by no person with beliefs that are the same

Greed and sin

mankind is not a revelation – cruel, corrupt, greedy and sinful
black is not black and white is not white
the default position of the deceitful
a perverse joke society has arranged by design
people will destroy a mind for money, thinking it's fine
their books of religion they carry for moral protection
dressed in best clothes on Sunday avoiding detection
the money they secretly save
they cannot take it beyond their grave
the next generation will spend laughing with contempt
they believe they are important in this society they play
if there is a God it will not save them as their families pray

The truth

I have seen the truth – the whole truth, nothing but the truth
clarity of mind, a sense of soul, integrity abound
never blurring word and sound
act with empathy seek the truth
show no contempt for transparency
faced with arrogance, pause – focus on accuracy
acting clever may be the way for others
I refuse to cross the imaginary line for that view
with disgust I refuse to lie to confuse the truth
other parties laugh – the truth buried in their lies
tomorrow, I remain a better man and just a little wise

PART 2

SHADES OF LOVE

Sky and clouds

staring at the sky today
the clouds formed a love heart
in the centre of the cloud – your name and number precise
this mosaic from heaven – I wonder how and why
mind calm I breathe a sigh
I thought nature had captured my heart
destined we would one day meet
I heard the echo of the birds wings fly by
I smiled – chosen to be your guy
a gust of wind – will my dream be blown away
as my mind captured this event
hoping your name remains clear to me
in my mind for eternity

Regina

seeing you for the first time, my smile a reflection in your eyes
I knew there was a beautiful connection making me wise
Regina long hair it is unfair
think of me Regina let me be you focus – your stare

your reflection in the mirror composed of grace
knowing a beautiful connection would take place
boys dream you are their desire
choose me Regina let me set your heart on fire

the girl down the road looks the part
if her name is not Regina it will break my heart
Regina has diamond eyes that sparkle – like cat eyes in the night
choose me Regina, let me pound your heart

Hearts and spirits

looking in your eyes deep in colour a surprise
sighing a breath of contentment in mutual silence
my dream was your dream you are special
your soul leading me into our world our life together
world of thoughts stay protected
world of urges unexposed remain uninfected
an electric aura our invisible shield
visionary thoughts never magnified with our dreams dignified
love is our eternity, hearts and spirits from different worlds
sincerity is our lifetime of hope

By design

by design I am me and you are you
you are small and I am tall
you are refined and I the comic fool
you are quiet and I am too
now we start the chain of love
censored by the spirit in the heaven above
amazing words smiles confuse the sight
acts of faith every night
my voice is loud and clear and new to you
we both stand strong
by design we admit no wrong
see you in heaven – by design

King and queen

when we are king and queen of the parish shire
we would be marching to our kingdom of desire
vibrant clapping is what you want to hear
our triumphant voices now so clear
virgin cows for the feast do not fear
let the people see us drunk with caskets of beer

commence the party with clowns our favourite songs
bring on the dancing girls with their leather throngs
bang the drum in the way you choose
rewind your mind and dance the blues

when we are king and queen, we will make the rules
we will have servants – the poor are such fools
listen subjects, my voice is the one to hear
I am the governing body that is clear

arrogance, evident just listen to the fake laughter
the masses to salute to me I am their master
pretend they are important to make them clap faster
bow to me in any weather I am their lord and paymaster

While you were out

while you were out, I daydreamed my mind to a trance so calm
while you were out, I prayed my favourite Old Testament Psalms

while you were out, I desired my pure thoughts of you
with my eyes closed I dreamed only for you – yes only of you, it's true

while you were out, I stared at all our pictures love trapped
behind the glass
while you were out, I drank my favourite blue vodka, my mask

while you were out, I played my favourite tunes on the piano in the
key of E
while you were out, I drank from bone china my favourite organic tea

while you were out, I told my friends they will be invited to
our love nest
while you were out, I informed them you are the best

Joe her dream

do me a favour Joe – she screamed today
pump me up and make me dirty your mind – let's play
you have been seen cruising about this town
that's what my girlfriends say

do me a favour Joe, – I want to show you my mind *(echo the word)*
I am not sure if it is as dirty as yours but it could be she smiled
it is yours to find *(echo the word)*
my torso is there for you I am a real bad girl today
let us walk the talk I have no more to say

inflated inside with your affection Joe she said – I just go very wild
do not distance our minds Joe, it's just amazing
I dreamt of a person like you Joe, since I was older than a child
it is been a while Joe we were at the altar – me as your bride

Swing honey

honey let us swing to the beat
it is exciting moving together in the heat
strip to our torso me lean, you curved for our bodies to meet
honey together the visual body – poetry is such a feat
show it to your girlfriends as they take their seat
do you agree now honey we are perfection of tattooed meat
the people in the crowd admiring our free visual treat
honey the cameras there filming as we swing to the beat

Broken robot

I am a broken robot with no mind, but I have a soul
I stare at my companion friend sharing my life such a pretty doll
I am a broken robot living in a toy box, but I have a soul
my pretty doll surprises everyone, when she caresses the broken robot, dancing the pole

I am the broken robot with my friend the pretty doll

crowds come to watch us when we do our primal dance
robotic movements transcend the crowd, to a total hypnotic trance
the papers and TV demand our sole attention to tell our story
we refuse, me the broken robot, her the pretty doll to expose our glory

I am the broken robot with my friend the pretty doll

we love each other too much these days
surrounded in our make believe world – harmless thoughts and ways
robotic movements by the broken robot and the pretty doll hypnotize and daze
dramatic movements confuse the minds of the onlookers
real people totally amazed

Mother and child

the baby sleeps so safe and sound
mother watching every breath carefully
heartbeats of both in perfect symmetry
devoid of worry with dreams, thoughts of desire
two minds interlocked as tight as secret steel wire
no one will ever hurt the baby or mother that is just love – plain
contentment in that room of trust and no disdain
never shout or scream to puncture the silence so serene
the tranquillity of love can be seen

Turn the key

turn the key to my heart and we will never part
lift my spirits and see me smile
rotate my head and with looks that would be smart
lower all expectations just for a while
run baby run chase the chase
go baby see it in your face
lipstick so red, limbs full of grace
breathe your breath like a steam train
cry your desire forget the pain
perspire your excitement for our gain
whisper your secret thoughts to make you sane
'remember me' in every way that makes your day
these are the only words I need to say

PART 3

REFLECTIONS OF THE MIND

Shut down our minds honey

past fun in the summer of English days
clouds in the sky, in my mind, to confuse memories of English days
the past brought down by memories gone stale the decant days
dark skies with clouds to confuse, bemuse, those fading ways
let's shut down our minds Regina honey

yesterday no fun the winter of Scandinavian days
rain in the sky, in my mind, to confuse memories of Scandinavian days
the past enhanced by memories gone stale those decant days
dark skies with clouds to confuse bemuse those fading ways
let's shut down our minds Helga honey

today again in the seasons of Australian days
sun in the sky, no clouds in my mind to confuse memories of past days
now transparent the past decant days
clear skies with no clouds to confuse bemuse those fading ways
let's not shut down our minds honey

You were a flower

I thought you were wise before the lies set in stone
now crack the veneer of shame and see what was lost
waiting to hear joy of past conversations
the laughter evaporated turned to a deep frost
you a flower, lost and petals fallen, life span doomed
withered and faded away
died before you fully bloomed
there were times in distant past
fun and games were designed to last
too late now, there is no time to wait
written in stone the concluding fate

Then and now

clouds weep in the summer haze
the rainbow appears to dazzle
piercing sun, eyes and mind confused like a psychotic maze
that was then this is now

reflect future enhanced no more in a mental haze
pretend smiles are real, laughter lines on a brow
eyes ringed, bloodshot with a dysfunctional glaze
that was then this is now

Betrayal and a thousand screams

betrayal and treachery is a violation
coins of silver a losers consolation

letter and words full of spite
pain created every night

enjoy a death of a thousand screams
after a life of jaundiced dreams

confused reality was normal for you
the author of lies too

childlike mentality – unable to smile to me
tortured soul of veneers for others not to see

looking for fame in a crowd of fools
trying to be a person of your Gods rules

playing to a captive crowd of six or seven
pretending, thinking you will go to heaven

what you achieved in your world of make believe
will never be part of my daydream
take with you, your evil schemes *(echo)*

Stupid man

I the stupid man
refused to listen to friends – believing they were fools
opened my mind, but I rejected the bad news
on reflection – sanity rules
I know these thoughts are true
when life gets so deep blue
pump me up with false dreams Doctor Joe
as my face declines a smile to a frown – I have to go

Dreams come true

on the bank, staring in a trance with a dusk sky
praying for hours the stream drifting
fragments of trees float past – I ask why

two eyes peering, the crocodile desiring food, will I die
staring back at that snout – he disappears, I sigh

my thoughts forge into a tainted fusion
your motives caused such confusion
counting non-existing clouds creates delusion
what you did deserves your life conclusion

throwing stones sink like my life gone without a trace
slowly eating lunch organic – wrapped in cotton lace
every crumb, not to waste
dreams come true knowing a true face

Peace

peace is in the air, I have no care
dramas of the past, memories not fair
listen carefully to what I have to say
treasure these words in your mind
it will be the final departing way

"look into my eyes free of lies – seeing the best
look into your heart – it will be your test
imagine all life being cool and calm
eternity being a dream – love, just be kind
there is peace in my heart and mind
go to pastures new
reap the benefits of silver coins
life is over with my view
scatter my ashes in the holy water
the hate in your heart, it is not wise
love a little – it will surprise
drink a cocktail –
love and hate called emotional fusion
becomes our toast and conclusion."

When truth was a gift

I salute you the queen hoarding the treasure
crime, the heads rolled today for your pleasure
there was a time I adored you – that was when truth was a gift

there is a torrent of blood flooding the stage creating a river
the axe is the power of the kingdom, the masses lips quiver
there was a time I would do anything for you
anything believe me it's so true – that was when truth was a gift

drag the corpses to the dogs to dismember the flesh so raw
the queen smirks departing from the red stage the people saw
there was a time I would cry for you
any time of day and day of the year – that was when truth was a gift

witness the saga of hell to scare me
there was a time I would die for you
in the darkest night of black so black – that was when truth was a gift

Evaporated love

evaporated love, conveyed in a nonchalant way
fun and hate, is the same whatever way you say
the silence of the night, I close my eyes and pray
hoping tomorrow is different from today
the future is bleak, come the month of May
games of summer bliss never again to play
empty of love is clear as the light of day
no memory, my statue made eroded in clay
take the money and run in your stylish way

Say goodbye

say goodbye – thought is in my head
never planned to say goodbye – before I am dead
you caused deep grief
the story of despair – you are the thought thief

my heart has no pain
the lack of truth makes me insane
wave your arms screaming with a stare
pretend to the people that care

life a game of dreadful dreams
make believe fun is not what it seems
creating a drama queen – is your façade
your human default to discard
no apologises for my view
knowing you're human too

PART 4

THE END AND BEYOND

Midnight blues

explosions within the brain
true – feel the pain
escape like the God of Troy
dreams mask emotions
firecrackers fierce expressions
imagine life – the other side
life is emotion dreams expired

In life there is air

live tomorrow with clear thoughts
a world of vanity, money a fleeting whim
ancient life stone tablet
engraved rules to win
never have to drink whisky or gin
in life there is air
the world decisions are unfair
conversations, debate that has no care
death nothing exists – do not despair
my soul I can see in there

The world I saw

I travelled the world east to west, north and south
coloured skins accents harsh soft from the mouth
religions (some) faked to control the masses what a mess
royalty prim consult their minders in expensive dress
images in my mind here to stay;
Alabama I originate from down south for the people unaware
Kentucky the bluegrass very green to stare
Florida swamps decadent people, beaches water warm, it's all there
Nigeria yam and rice nice but no clean water – that ain't fair
Channel Islands a place of small bays and rough sea, beware
London thousand miles away imagine crowds so close to touch
Swiss Alp white capped mountains focused – too much
Canadian vast wheat plain – to my mind what a bore
New Zealand in an ocean wild, hot gases exploding from the floor
Australian outback lands flat, ancient rock and ground dark red
Sydney bikini clad darlings, a veneer of health alive not dead

It's over my friend

it's over my friend when the lights go out and the beat goes quiet

if I climb a hill so near but far, I am sure you will understand – you might

maybe the drums will roll, maybe the heads will sway

only time will tell, wait for that religious bell on this day

it's over my friend, let's get that straight

it's over my friend, the pall bearer proceeds through the gate

it's over my friend, when the sun goes down and the winds cascade away

I will make amends next time around – I promise, believe what I say

I did make mistakes, that is fair to say each and every day

I will try my best next time around, I apologise to all, I tried it my way

it's over my friend when the thin crowds depart – is that the norm

wet and drenched in a flash tropical storm

footprints deep in the mud, all the memories about our strife

heartbreaks so big, in this fragile wasted life

The last soldier falls

the bugle plays the requiem for the fallen soldier, far away shores
not in the church, what music will they play
content to hear a tune silent, this autumn month of May
remember in your mind laughter at times, so kind I must say
I a soldier in my mind, fighting battles my way
oblivious to loved ones, fought everyday
next time, I try to make things better the only way
meditate for me thoughts your memories as you pray
friends, don't cry for me a sad moment for you today
it's acceptable to wipe the few tears away
the soldier falls it's over for me now as at today
nothing more to say or do until we meet another day

True is not blue

thoughts will not take me to heaven high above the blue
recover from despair hidden from my friends view
granted a pardon to find a great person like you?
now I plan my departure that is my goal
the Buddhist will be there to chant songs of prayer
in Nepal there will be people to calm the soul
fame was for others dreaming like fools not true
return to my maker next time – may not be so blue
reincarnation is the saviour for you too

Prelude of the end

lying still, not alone, breathing so slowly
in the shade eyes closed I still see your image, sad to say
my heartbeat slows thoughts cascade away

water from the glass touches my lips from the hand of love
in the room I hear the nurse whisper I must stay
a soft warm hand brushes my face I touch then it moves away

the perfume I discern an aroma my senses decline today
where is she I mumble, as my eyes finally close?
do not cry for me, my three darlings, I mumble as I fade away

Life

life is finding one's true soul – attempting to be that person
a surprise when one finds the secret with wide eyes
money stacked in the bank, drama queens, seeking diversion
the sacred flock will preach, the meek will inherit these lies
a journey time past, hoping to meet the good people
a shame the reality and the fiction cannot meet to discuss the past
with a parting smile as the last gasp is exhaled
if I am correct the joke will be on the other's lives that did not last

Beyond the stars

look up in the night sky and see the stars
look to heaven and it seems far past Mars
close my eyes I dream of all good things to be
it's so comforting to see a reflection of God in front of me

amazed at the pattern of the bright night stars
Southern Cross piercing the sky somewhere up there near Mars
listen carefully I hear the silence which has called me, it has to be
it's just so comforting, the image of the God waiting for me

I left behind my family, the solitude in my soul beyond those stars
it is so silent in heaven, so far just past Mars
now smile my family and friends my memory is for you all to see
I loved you so much, remember that, when you think of me

Seeing

I see what you see
you see what I see
but do we see what others see
seeing may be learning
seeing may be believing
but at the end of the day it's just intimidating
now surge forward and see the beyond over the sky
now leap backwards and see the atmosphere below the sky
the soul has gone and I do not know where or why

Pagan

a Pagan world they worship – in the book
cold, you recall soul memories in that world to digest
is the Pagan world better than we endured?
in a world full of shame and pain, deceit
people divisive, failing to assist mankind – me – a mortal
a game to play each day – so strange
thinking of the ancient Pagan to pray
rescued by my God comforting each day

The end – goodbye this world

www.ingramcontent.com/pod-product-compliance
Lightning Source LLC
Chambersburg PA
CBHW071543080526
44588CB00011B/1772